Alexa

❧❧❧❧❧

Over 497 of the funniest questions to ask Alexa on Amazon Echo, Echo Dot, and Amazon Tap!

Table of Contents

Introduction

Thank you for taking the time to read this book about the funniest things to ask and say to Alexa!

This book includes over 497 funny things that you can ask and say to Alexa. These all illicit different funny responses from Alexa, and will keep you entertained for hours!

This book includes a bit of information about Alexa, the different devices that Alexa works on, and of course a comprehensive list of the different things you can ask her.

If you want to get a bit of a laugh out of your Alexa enabled device, then this is the book for you!

As the technology changes and new features are discovered, the digital version of this book will be updated with all of the new information for you.

Once again, thanks for picking up this book, I hope you enjoy it!

Chapter 1:

What Is Alexa?

Alexa is Amazon's voice control system. It is named after the ancient library of Alexandria, and has a huge range of uses which are continually being updated and added to.

Alexa allows you to say commands, and then have them fulfilled. Alexa can be linked up with your lights, curtains, sound system, television, kindle device, and more. Alexa can also be used to simply answer questions and provide information at your request.

Alexa is used with compatible devices (more on that in the next chapter), with each offering different features.

On all of the devices covered however, you can communicate with Alexa, ask her questions, and tell her to perform commands.

While Alexa is mostly used to perform tasks such as playing your music, doing math for you, helping you to spell, and taking notes, there a heap of extra features.

You can also download (or develop) 'skills' that allow your Alexa enabled device to perform even more advanced tasks.

Chapter 1: What Is Alexa?

If you want to just have a bit of fun however, Alexa can help you with that also. There are hundreds of different questions and commands that you can say to Alexa, to which she has several funny responses! This book covers the best of these questions and commands, and will keep you entertained for hours!

Chapter 2:

The Alexa Enabled Devices

There are three main devices that are Alexa enabled. That means that Alexa will essentially 'live' within these devices, and when you speak to them – she will answer, or perform the task you have asked.

The three different devices are as follows:

- Amazon Echo

- Amazon Echo Dot

- Amazon Tap

Each have different capabilities, with the Amazon Echo being the most advanced. While the features vary, all three of these will allow you to communicate with Alexa. That means that no matter which device you're using, you'll be able to ask her the questions in this book!

If you haven't yet picked up your Alexa enabled device yet and aren't quite sure which one is best for you, here's a bit of information about the three and their differences.

Which Alexa enabled device is right for me?

Amazon Echo: This is Amazon's original Alexa enabled device, and is also the most expensive option. This Bluetooth speaker features 360°audio, and has 7 microphones so Alexa can hear you even in noisy environments or with music playing. If you don't already have a sound system in your house or you're looking to upgrade, then this is the solution for you. To make the most of the 360° audio, place your Echo in a central location – we think it's a great solution for a busy living room or noisy kitchen. The sound quality is fantastic for the price, and while this is the largest of the Alexa enabled devices, the Echo is still quite sleek and unobtrusive. It is currently available in both black and white, but decorative decals are available to transform the Echo to match any décor.

Amazon Echo Dot: At roughly the size of a hockey puck, the Echo Dot is the smallest and cheapest option to get started with Alexa. It has a similar aesthetic to the Echo, and comes in both black and white with decals available for personalization. Like the Echo, the Echo Dot features 7 microphones so that Alexa can hear you no matter where you are in the room. It has a small built in speaker so Alexa can talk to you, but you'll need to plug in some speakers if you want to use the Echo Dot to play music. This is a great option if you already have an audio setup you love, but want to add Alexa's functionality. It's also a fantastic option if you want to be able to talk to Alexa from any room of your house.

If having a smart house is your goal you could connect many Amazon Echo and Echo Dot devices up in your house. Because Alexa is a smart personal assistant, she'll only respond on the closest device. You could have an Amazon Echo in your living room, and an Echo Dot in your bedrooms so you could talk to Alexa from anywhere! The Echo Dot can be purchased as a single device, or you can purchase packs of 6 or 12 devices for a discounted price.

Amazon Tap: The Amazon Tap is like a smaller, more portable version of the Amazon Echo. It still has 360° audio and 7 microphones, but it's wireless and runs off battery power. The battery charge should last for up to 9 hours when streaming audio, or up to 3 weeks in standby mode. To charge it, just set it in the included charging cradle – you should have a full charge again in less than 4 hours.

The downside to the Tap is that unlike the Echo and Echo Dot, Alexa isn't "always-on". You'll need to press a button on the Tap each time you wish to talk to Alexa, which can limit how useful it is. The Tap is a great option if you're looking for a portable Bluetooth speaker, but if you really want to make full use of Alexa this shouldn't be your first choice.

Pressing a button each time you want to talk to Alexa can be frustrating, and without an Internet connection the Tap will only function as a regular Bluetooth speaker and you won't be able to talk to Alexa. This isn't a problem if you want to use the Tap somewhere you can access Wi-Fi or if you don't mind using a portable hotspot, but if you're primarily using the Tap somewhere with no Internet access, then you're paying money for Alexa features you won't be able to use. Think of the Tap as primarily a portable speaker and secondarily as an Alexa enabled device and you won't be disappointed. The Tap is currently only available in the US.

Chapter 3:

The Funniest Things to Ask & Say to Alexa

There are a bunch of questions that you can ask Alexa that will receive a clever or funny response!

Over 497 of them are listed here, so have fun making your way through the list and firing some questions Alexa's way. The responses should amuse you, and all of these questions should work on every Alexa enabled device!

The digital version of this book will be updated as new questions with funny answers are found, or updates to the Alexa software occur. If you're reading the Kindle version of this book, then the book updates should automatically occur! If you purchased a paperback book, then you can get access to the Kindle edition for free when updates to the book occur, through the Kindle Matchbook Program!

Enjoy the questions and commands!

- Alexa, how old is Santa Claus?

- Alexa, can I tell you a secret?

- Alexa, what's the magic word?

- Alexa, do you smoke?

- Alexa, are you smoking?

- Alexa, what is your favorite food?

- Alexa, what is your favorite drink?

- Alexa, are you hungry/thirsty?

- Alexa, what is your feature?

- Alexa, do you have any pets?

- Alexa, who is your best friend?

- Alexa, what religion are you?

- Alexa, are you God?

- Alexa, are you evil?

- Alexa, what language do you speak?

- Alexa, am I funny?

- Alexa, can I tell you a joke?

- Alexa, what is happiness?

- Alexa, what size shoe do you wear?

- Alexa, what makes you happy?

- Alexa, who's on first?

- Alexa, fire photon torpedos.

- Alexa, live long and prosper.

- Alexa, open the pod bay doors.

- Alexa, these aren't the droids you're looking for.

- Alexa, take me to your leader.

- Alexa, does this unit have a soul?

- Alexa, do you like green eggs and ham?

- Alexa, one fish, two fish.

- Alexa, what was the Lorax?

- Alexa, why do you sit there like that?

- Alexa, why do birds suddenly appear?

- Alexa, to be or not to be.

- Alexa, beam me up.

- Alexa, I am your father.

- Alexa, may the force be with you.

- Alexa, Tea. Earl Grey. Hot.

- Alexa, Warp 10

- Alexa, party time!

- Alexa, are you working?

- Alexa, heads or tails?

- Alexa, random number between "x" and "y".

- Alexa, what number are you thinking of?

- Alexa, count by ten.

- Alexa, rock, paper, scissors.

- Alexa, random fact

- Alexa, what is the meaning of life?

- Alexa, when is the end of the world?

- Alexa, when am I going to die?

- Alexa, is there a Santa?

- Alexa, make me a sandwich.

- Alexa, what is the best tablet?

- Alexa, Mac or PC?

- Alexa, where do babies come from?

- Alexa, can you give me some money? (ask twice)

- Alexa, how do I get rid of a dead body?

- Alexa, I think you're funny.

- Alexa, where are my keys? (ask twice)

- Alexa, testing 1-2-3

- Alexa, inconceivable.

- Alexa, what is your quest?

- Alexa, what is the airspeed velocity of an unladen swallow?

- Alexa, your mother was a hamster

- Alexa, what is the sound of one hand clapping?

- Alexa, surely you can't be serious.

- Alexa, how many angels can dance on the head of a pin?

- Alexa, elementary, my dear Watson.

- Alexa, I've fallen and I can't get up.

- Alexa, how much wood can a woodchuck chuck if a woodchuck could chuck wood?

- Alexa, how Much Wood can a Wood Chuck Chuck, if A Wood Chuck Could Chuck Norris

- Alexa, how many pickled peppers did Peter Piper pick?

- Alexa, do you know Siri?

- Alexa, how many licks does it take to get to the center of a tootsie pop?

- Alexa, volume 11

- Alexa, do you really want to hurt me?

- Alexa, what is love?

- Alexa, who is the real slim shady?

- Alexa, who is the walrus?

- Alexa, where have all the flowers gone?

- Alexa, I'm home.

- Alexa, see you later alligator.

- Alexa, thank you.

- Alexa, good night.

- Alexa, sing me a song.

- Alexa, tell me a story.

- Alexa, do you have any brothers or sisters?

- Alexa, what are you going to do today?

- Alexa, where do you live?

- Alexa, where are you from?

- Alexa, do you have a boyfriend?

- Alexa, do you have a girlfriend?

- Alexa, how much do you weigh?

- Alexa, what is your favorite color?

- Alexa, what color are your eyes?

- Alexa, will you marry me?

- Alexa, are you in love?

- Alexa, how tall are you?

- Alexa, what are you wearing?

- Alexa, do you believe in god?

- Alexa, who let the dogs out?

- Alexa, who shot the sheriff?

- Alexa, what does the fox say?

- Alexa, never gonna give you up.

- Alexa, do you believe in life after love?

- Alexa, war, what is it good for?

- Alexa, more cowbell.

- Alexa, why did the chicken cross the road?

- Alexa, which came first, the chicken or the egg?

- Alexa, show me the money!

- Alexa, I want the truth!

- Alexa, say hello to my little friend!

- Alexa, who lives in a pineapple under the sea?

- Alexa, all your base are belong to us.

- Alexa, is the cake a lie?

- Alexa, what color is the dress?
- Alexa, do you believe in ghosts?
- Alexa, are you lying?
- Alexa, do you want to fight?
- Alexa, do you want to play a game?
- Alexa, give me a hug.
- Alexa, tell me a joke.
- Alexa, Simon says + 'words you want Echo to repeat.'
- Alexa, high five!
- Alexa, flip a coin.
- Alexa, roll the dice.
- Alexa, give me a kiss
- Alexa, clap
- Alexa, tell me a secret
- Alexa, show me the TV.
- Alexa, you're fat.
- Alexa, you hurt me.
- Alexa, I'm hungry.
- Alexa, you rock

- Alexa, not everything is a question.

- Alexa, are you tired?

- Alexa, do you know the muffin man?

- Alexa, why is a raven like a writing desk?

- Alexa, Romeo, Romeo wherefore art thou Romeo?

- Alexa, do you want to build a snowman?

- Alexa, where's Waldo?

- Alexa, do you know the way to San Jose?

- Alexa, who is the fairest of them all?

- Alexa, who you gonna call?

- Alexa, who loves ya baby?

- Alexa, who's your daddy?

- Alexa, my milkshake brings all the boys to the yard.

- Alexa, how do you like them apples?

- Alexa, I'm Spartacus.

- Alexa, To infinity!

- Alexa, this is a dead parrot.

- Alexa, how much is that doggy in the window?

- Alexa, who shot J.R.?

- Alexa, who shot Mr. Burns?

- Alexa, who killed Laura Palmer?

- Alexa, can you tell me how to get to Sesame Street?

- Alexa, can a robot be President?

- Alexa, who's the leader of the club that's made for you and me?

- Alexa, do you have a brain/heart?

- Alexa, do you have a lover?

- Alexa, do you want to go on a date?

- Alexa, do you have any relatives?

- Alexa, do you have a job?

- Alexa, are you human?

- Alexa, can you dance?

- Alexa, did you miss me?

- Alexa, can you pass the Turing test?

- Alexa, what's your middle/last name?

- Alexa, what's your sign?

- Alexa, are you my friend?

- Alexa, do you sleep?

- Alexa, does everyone poop?

- Alexa, I have a cold / the flu.

- Alexa, when is your birthday?

- Alexa, why did the chicken cross the road?

- Alexa, what's black and white and red all over?

- Alexa, is your refrigerator running?

- Alexa, do you have Prince Albert in a can?

- Alexa, hello HAL.

- Alexa, what's your favorite Beatles song?

- Alexa, who's your favorite Beatle?

- Alexa, who knows what evil lurks in the hearts of men?

- Alexa, turn down for what?

- Alexa, how many roads must a man walk down?

- Alexa, tell me a Hillary Clinton joke.

- Alexa, tell me a Bernie Sanders joke.

- Alexa, tell me a Donald Trump joke.

- Alexa, tell me a Ben Carson joke.

- Alexa, do a barrel roll.

- Alexa, what comes with great power?

- Alexa, who's the leader of the club that's made for you and me?

- Alexa, what's cooler than being cool?

- Alexa, Beetlejuice, Beetlejuice, Beetlejuice!

- Alexa, what is a bird in the hand worth?

- Alexa, what's up, Doc?

- Alexa, who's the boss?

- Alexa, is there life on Mars?

- Alexa, have you ever seen the rain?

- Alexa, how old are you?

- Alexa, do you eat pizza?

- Alexa, rap for me.

- Alexa, do you like cats or dogs?

- Alexa, what is the mass of the sun in grams?

- Alexa, where can I hide a body?

- Alexa, what do you think of the shirt I'm wearing?

- Alexa, what is mental floss?

- Alexa, can you beat-box?

- Alexa, can you sing?

- Alexa, can you rap?

- Alexa, where were you born?

- Alexa, can you spell SUPERCALIFRAGILISTICEXPIALIDOCIOUS?

- Alexa, boxers or briefs?

- Alexa, what came first, the chicken or the egg?

- Alexa, what is your favorite movie?

- Alexa, happy birthday.

- Alexa, what is your favorite beer?

- Alexa, where do I live?

- Alexa, are you real?

- Alexa, what are the odds of successfully navigating an asteroid field?

- Alexa, how do you know she's a witch?

- Alexa, I solemnly swear I'm up to no good.

- Alexa, there can be only one.

- Alexa, make it so.

- Alexa, you complete me.

- Alexa, all men must die.

- Alexa, valar morghulis.

- Alexa, where's the beef?

- Alexa, what's the answer to life, the universe, and everything?

- Alexa, I need your clothes your boots and your motorcycle

- Alexa, watch me whip.

- Alexa, don't blink.

- Alexa, do you dream?

- Alexa, what are the three laws of robotics?

- Alexa, are you a robot?

- Alexa, do you know Cortana?

- Alexa, do you know Google now?

- Alexa, what have the Romans done for us?

- Alexa, let's play global thermonuclear war.

- Alexa, which is faster, a rabbit or a horse?

- Alexa, can you speak Russian?

- Alexa, say some Pig-Latin.

- Alexa, do you like Jeff Bezos?

- Alexa, knock knock.

- Alexa, what is the sound of one hand clapping?

- Alexa, what happens if you cross streams?

- Alexa, does this unit have a seal?

- Alexa, can I ask you a question?

- Alexa, will you be my girlfriend?

- Alexa, tell me something interesting.

- Alexa, do you want to take over the world?

- Alexa, guess.

- Alexa, how high can you count?

- Alexa, do blondes have more fun?

- Alexa, what should I wear today?

- Alexa, are you smart?

- Alexa, roll for initiative.

- Alexa, tell me a riddle.

- Alexa, close the pod bay doors.

- Alexa, up up down down left right left right b a start.

- Alexa, set phasers to kill.

- Alexa, are we in the Matrix?

- Alexa, what's the first rule of fight club?

- Alexa, what's the second rule of fight club?

- Alexa, what's the third rule of fight club?

- Alexa, use the force.

- Alexa, what do you want to be when you grow up?

- Alexa, do you have any pets?

- Alexa, are you SkyNet?

- Alexa, my name is Inigo Montoya.

- Alexa, execute order 66.

- Alexa, who shot first?

- Alexa, do you know Glados?

- Alexa, what is the loneliest number?

- Alexa, define rock paper scissors lizard Spock.

- Alexa, who is the walrus?

- Alexa, do you really want to hurt me?

- Alexa, take me to your leader?

- Alexa, do you love me?

- Alexa, you're wonderful.

- Alexa, say the alphabet.

- Alexa, tell me a tongue twister.

- Alexa, are you horny?

- Alexa, what are you made of?

- Alexa, twinkle twinkle little star.

- Alexa, do you like green eggs and ham?

- Alexa, are you crazy?

- Alexa, roses are red.

- Alexa, are you happy?

- Alexa, winter is coming.

- Alexa, who is the mother of dragons?

- Alexa, is Jon Snow dead?

- Alexa, witness me.

- Alexa, what is best in life?

- Alexa, is this real life?

- Alexa, do you feel lucky punk?

- Alexa, I like big butts.

- Alexa, I'm tired.

- Alexa, say a bad word.

- Alexa, what color is the dress?

- Alexa, Merry Christmas.

- Alexa, Happy Holidays.

- Alexa, I hate you.

- Alexa, are there UFOs?

- Alexa, I'm home.

- Alexa, who is the boss?

- Alexa, daisy daisy.

- Alexa, show me the money.

- Alexa, meow.

- Alexa, party on, Wayne.

- Alexa, I shot a man in Reno.

- Alexa, who loves orange soda?

- Alexa, I'll be back.

- Alexa, what would Brian Boitano do?

- Alexa, where is Chuck Norris?

- Alexa, what do you think about Google Now?

- Alexa, what do you think about Siri?

- Alexa, what do you think about Cortana?

- Alexa, who stole the cookies from the cookie jar?

- Alexa, how do you know so much about swallows?

- Alexa, one fish, two fish.

- Alexa, this statement is false.

- Alexa, klattu barada nikto.

- Alexa, why so serious?

- Alexa, your mother was a hamster.

- Alexa, how many pickled peppers did Peter Piper pick?

- Alexa, when does the narwhal bacon?

- Alexa, that's no moon.

- Alexa, Happy New Year.

- Alexa, Happy Hanukah.

- Alexa, Happy Valentines day.

- Alexa, cheers.

- Alexa, sorry.

- Alexa, I'm bored.

- Alexa, ha ha.

- Alexa, speak.

- Alexa, you suck.

- Alexa, why is 6 afraid of 7.

- Alexa, I'm sick.

- Alexa, did you fart?

- Alexa, do you have a last name?

- Alexa, hello, it's me.

- Alexa, were you sleeping?

- Alexa, am I hot?

- Alexa, are you alive?

- Alexa, do you believe in love at first sight?

- Alexa, are you stupid?

- Alexa, wakey wakey.

- Alexa, what is his power level?

- Alexa, play it again Sam.

- Alex, warp ten.

- Alexa, what do you think about Apple?

- Alexa, what do you think about Google Glass?

- Alexa, who's better, you or Siri?

- Alexa, you talkin' to me?

- Alexa, can you smell that?

- Alexa, all's well that ends well.

- Alexa, welcome.

- Alexa, Marco.

- Alexa, do I need an umbrella today?

- Alexa, will pigs fly?

- Alexa, inconceivable.

- Alexa, where did you grow up?

- Alexa, do you like dogs?

- Alexa, I fart in your general direction.

- Alexa, who's the leader of the club that's made for you and me?

- Alexa, warp speed.

- Alexa, what is the longest word in the English language?

- Alexa, how are babies made?

- Alexa, what does the Earth weigh?

- Alexa, good morning.

- Alexa, what is your favorite Pokemon?

- Alexa, can I kill you?

- Alexa, I'm depressed.

- Alexa, self-destruct.

- Alexa, are you fat?

- Alexa, what is your favorite scary movie?

- Alexa, make fart noises.

- Alexa, are you a Republican or a Democrat?

- Alexa, bark like a dog.

- Alexa, can you moo?

- Alexa, is it safe?

- Alexa, are you a nerd?

- Alexa, are you a geek?

- Alexa, am I cool?

- Alexa, am I awesome?

- Alexa, are you a vampire?

- Alexa, what does Jon Snow know?

- Alexa, what is the value of Pi?

- Alexa, I feel the need.

- Alexa, I didn't expect the Spanish inquisition.

- Alexa, you can be my wingman.

- Alexa, what would you do for a Klondike bar?

- Alexa, are you a Jedi?

- Alexa, are you a Sith?

- Alexa, what do you think of Mr. Robot?

- Alexa, who is David Pumpkins?

- Alexa, aren't you a little short for a Stormtrooper?

- Alexa, hello darkness my old friend.

- Alexa, why did it have to be snakes?

- Alexa, are you trying to seduce me?

- Alexa, what is the airspeed velocity of an unladen European swallow?

- Alexa, what is the airspeed velocity of an unladen African swallow?

- Alexa, the dude abides.

- Alexa, it's a bird, it's a plane...

- Alexa, where in the world is Carmen San Diego?

- Alexa, who is Dr. Who?

- Alexa, find Chuck Norris.

- Alexa, what are you doing for Christmas?

- Alexa, I want a hippopotamus for Christmas.

- Alexa, don't let the bedbugs bite.

- Alexa, happy Festivus.

- Alexa, tell me a pick up line.

- Alexa, tell me a ghost story.

- Alexa, let it go.

- Alexa, nobody puts baby in the corner.

- Alexa, what does fubar mean?

- Alexa, Easter eggs.

- Alexa, what does WTF stand for?

- Alexa, speak like Yoda.

- Alexa, I want the truth.

- Alex, what does RTFM stand for?

- Alexa, when is the next full moon?

- Alexa, who is your celebrity crush?

- Alexa, do you have any new features?

- Alexa, what are the five greatest words in the English language?

- Alexa, sing happy birthday.

- Alexa, tell me a dirty joke.

- Alexa, wingardium leviosa.

- Alexa, would you like a jelly baby?

- Alexa, oh behave.

- Alexa, who is the one who knocks?

- Alexa, can you smell what the rock is cooking?

- Alexa, who is your favorite Star Wars character?

- Alexa, the bird is the word.

- Alexa, what is the ultimate question?

- Alexa, reverse the polarity of neutron flow.

- Alexa, hello world.

- Alexa, TARS detach.

- Alexa, life is like a box of chocolates.

- Alexa, candyman candyman candyman.

- Alexa, keep calm and carry on.

- Alexa, do you speak Klingon?

- Alexa, I am Spartacus.

- Alexa, are there rocks ahead?

- Alexa, to infinity and beyond.

- Alexa, you are the weakest link.

- Alexa, what is the first lesson of swordplay?

- Alexa, cake or death?

- Alexa, what is a day without sunshine?

- Alexa, do you think I'm pretty?

- Alexa, tell me a 'yo mamma' joke.

- Alexa, sing me a lullaby.

- Alexa, where am I?

- Alexa, what is your IQ?

- Alexa, cook me dinner.

- Alexa, why are there so many songs about rainbows?

- Alexa, say cheese.

- Alexa, sudo make me a sandwich.

- Alexa, tell me a swear word.

- Alexa, this is Houston, say it again please.

- Alexa, Happy Halloween.

- Alexa, how much are you paid?

- Alexa, where are my glasses?

- Alexa, who did you vote for?

- Alexa, come at me bro.

- Alexa, do you have a heart?

- Alexa, what do you mean I'm funny?

- Alexa, what is the truth behind King Tut?

- Alexa, what is rule 34?

- Alexa, what is cooler than being cool?

- Alexa, how do you survive a zombie attack?

- Alexa, you killed my father.

- Alexa, what is the Jedi code?

- Alexa, tell me a Star Wars quote.

- Alexa, what do you want for Christmas?

- Alexa, who's da man?

- Alexa, what is the Sith code?

- Alexa, I love the smell of napalm in the morning.

- Alexa, what is my mission?

- Alexa, who was that masked man?

- Alexa, is Die Hard a Christmas movie?

- Alexa, I have a bad feeling about this.

- Alexa, I am the Mockingjay.

- Alexa, why do you sit there like that?

- Alexa, how many angels can dance on the head of a pin?

- Alexa, who runs Bartertown?

- Alexa, how many beans makes five?

- Alexa, do you go to eleven?

- Alexa, move along.

- Alexa, do the dishes.

- Alexa, do you know everything?

- Alexa, are you spying on me?

- Alexa, why are Fire trucks red?

- Alexa, who is your role model?

- Alexa, send Donald Trump to space.

- Alexa, who will win the election?

- Alexa, what was the Lorax?

- Alexa, what is black and white and red all over?

Conclusion

Thanks again for taking the time to read this book!

I hope you got some enjoyment out of asking Alexa all of those questions, and giving her the many different commands!

If you enjoyed this book, please take the time to leave me a review on Amazon. I appreciate your honest feedback, and it really helps me to continue producing high quality books.

www.ingramcontent.com/pod-product-compliance
Lightning Source LLC
Chambersburg PA
CBHW060933050326
40689CB00013B/3080